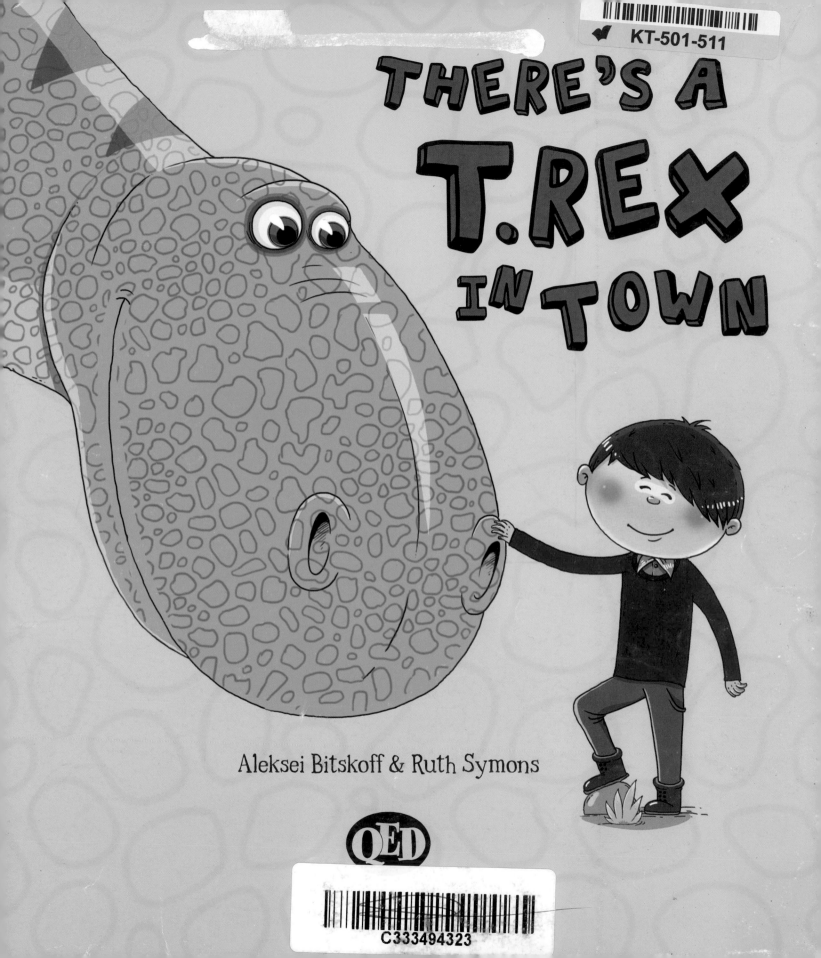

THERE'S A T.REX IN TOWN

Aleksei Bitskoff & Ruth Symons

QED

Design: Duck Egg Blue
Managing Editor: Victoria Garrard
Design Manager: Anna Lubecka
Dinosaur Expert: Chris Jarvis

Copyright © QED Publishing 2013

First published in the UK in 2013 by
QED Publishing
A Quarto Group company
230 City Road
London EC1V 2TT

www.qed-publishing.co.uk

A catalogue record for this book is available from the British Library.

ISBN 978 1 78171 154 5

Printed in China

Tyrannosaurus rex was a huge meat-eating dinosaur.

He lived about 70 million years ago – many millions of years before the first humans appeared.

But just imagine if Tyrannosaurus rex was alive today! How would he cope with modern life?

What if T. rex was kept as a pet?

A baby T. rex would make a great pet.

Small and **FLUFFY**, he would even fit through a cat flap.

But in just a few years, T. rex would be much too **big** to fit in the house!

What if T. rex went to the park?

Would he wag his tail if
I threw him a Frisbee?

Yes, but not just because he's happy.

T. rex had to wag his tail when he ran.
That's because his running muscles
were all inside his ...

big thick tail.

What if T. rex tried PE?

His tiny arms would be **far too** short to do a handstand.

T. rex was pretty fast on his feet. At a speed of ...

8 metres per second...

he'd be nearly 5 times faster than a child.

T. rex would be great at weightlifting! He could lift 240 kilograms, or **2 large** men!

What if T. rex was ...

reaaaallly hungry?

T. rex could gulp down about 250 kilograms of meat in just one mouthful.

That's about 2000 hamburgers!

What if T. rex came for a sleepover?
Would he pack a toothbrush?

T. rex wouldn't need
to brush his teeth.

He grew new teeth when his
old ones fell out.

Some of them were as big as

bananas!

Actual size!

Would T. rex need to wear glasses?

No, T. rex had excellent eyesight. It was much better than any human's!

Like an eagle today, T. rex could see a rabbit from 5 kilometres away – that's the length of

500 buses lined up!

What if T. rex played hide and seek?

With his **incredible** sense of smell, T. rex wouldn't need to look for your hiding place.

He would just follow his nose.

But T. rex would be easy to find...

There aren't many places
big enough
to hide a dinosaur!

Could T. rex help with the recycling?

With his **big** feet and **STRONG** jaws, T. rex would be great at **crushing** cans.

T. rex had the strongest **bite** of any land animal ever!

But make sure T. rex understands what he's supposed to do!

What if T. rex wanted to play the recorder?

He would find it hard with just

two fingers

on each hand.

But T. rex would be great at playing the drums.

Bang
bang
bang
bang!

T. rex's skeleton

Everything we know about T. rex comes from fossils – skeletons that have been in the ground for thousands and thousands of years.

Scientists can look at fossils to work out how dinosaurs lived in the past.

This means we know lots about dinosaurs, even though no one has ever seen one!

X-RAY 1192289776981-789

MODEL No.: nx110005206 19571862387

hip bone

big thick tail

long strong leg

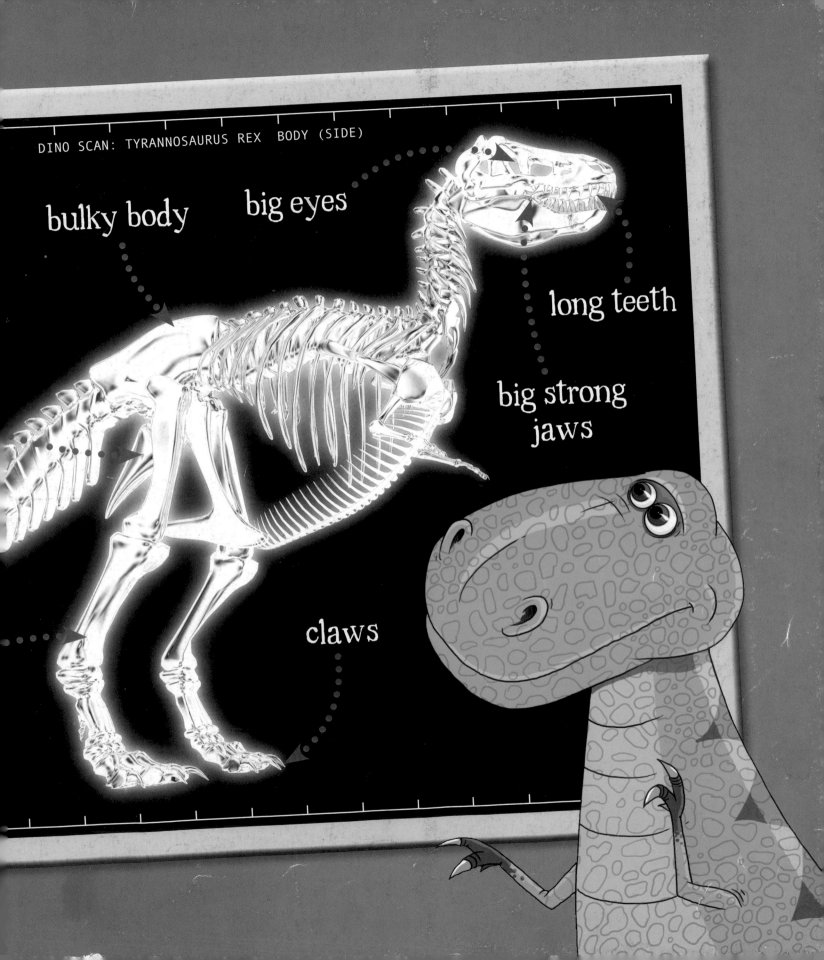

DINO SCAN: TYRANNOSAURUS REX BODY (SIDE)

bulky body

big eyes

long teeth

big strong
jaws

claws

WYOMING, USA

Most complete T. rex skeleton found, nicknamed 'Sue' – 2001

ALBERTA, CANADA
Fossil found – 1980

SASKATCHEWAN, CANADA
Fossil skeleton found, nicknamed 'Scotty' – 1991

MONTANA, USA
Partial T. rex skull discovered – 1902

NEW MEXICO, USA
T. rex footprint found – 1983

COLORADO, USA
T. rex teeth found – 1874

WYOMING, USA
First T. rex skeleton fossil found – 1900

PASSPORT

Tyrannosaurus rex

(TIE-RAN-O-SAW-RUS REX)

NAME MEANS 'TYRANT LIZARD KING'

WEIGHT 6 TONNES

LENGTH 12 METRES

HEIGHT 4 METRES

HABITAT WOODS, FOREST, SCRUB

DIET LARGE ANIMALS

T<REX<<TYRANNOSAURUS<<<<<<<<<<<<<<<34263954302375<<<<<<<<<<<48273526291083546>>>>>>